The Purple Muncher

Written by Paul Shipton

Illustrated by Kimberley Pope

Josh and Ella were playing in the garden. "Don't go far," said Josh's uncle. "It will be time for lunch soon."

Josh didn't feel like eating lunch.
"What's wrong?" Ella asked.
"My uncle's lamb curry is horrible!" Josh said.

Just then there was a sound.
A little spaceship was in the garden.

A purple thing with tentacles shuffled
out of the spaceship.
"Who are you?" asked Ella.
"The Purple Muncher," said the thing.

With one tentacle it grabbed an apple from
the tree.
"Food!" it cried.
It gobbled the apple in under a second.

"I need food!" cried The Purple Muncher.
Its tummy gurgled.
Josh unwrapped a bit of bubblegum.

The Purple Muncher grabbed the
bubblegum and began to chew.
It dribbled on its chin. Then it gulped.
"You don't EAT bubblegum!" said Ella.

The Purple Muncher's tummy rumbled.
"I need food!" it cried.
"I can't get food for you," said Josh.

The Purple Muncher grabbed Mum's bicycle
and began to eat!
"That's impossible!" cried Ella.

But Ella was wrong.
The Purple Muncher ate every little bit
and finished with a burp.
It gnashed its teeth. "I NEED FOOD!"

It started eating the apple tree.
"Don't!" cried Josh.
But The Purple Muncher went on eating.

"This is terrible!" said Ella. "Is it going to eat the house next? Then the town? Then the Earth? What can we do?"

"I know!" said Josh.
He ran into the house. Five seconds later he was back with a bowl.
"Try this," he said.

The Purple Muncher reached out a
tentacle and took the bowl.
It had a nibble, then shouted, "YUCK!
HORRIBLE!"

It climbed back to the spaceship and zoomed off.

"See?" said Josh with a smile. "I told you my uncle's lamb curry is terrible!"